Live Action

Swimming

Andrew Langley

Chrysalis Education

Distributed in the United States by
Smart Apple Media
2140 Howard Drive West
North Mankato, Minnesota 56003

Library of Congress Control Number: 2003116867

ISBN 1-59389-151-2

Editorial Manager: Joyce Bentley
Project Editors: Lionel Bender and Clare Lewis
Designer: Ben White
Production: Kim Richardson
Picture Researcher: Cathy Stastny

Produced by Bender Richardson White, U.K.

Printed in China

10 9 8 7 6 5 4 3 2 1

Words in **bold** can be found in Words to remember on page 31.

Picture credits
Corbis: 1, 6 (Paul A. Souders), 10 (Mark Gamba), 11 (Ralph A. Clevenger), 19, 21, 23.
Digital Vision: 13, 15, 20, 24. Rex Features Ltd: 7 (Phanie Agency), 8 (James D. Morgan),
9 (Chris Martin Bahr), 12 (Action Press), 14 (Sunset), 17 (Ted Blackbrow), 22 (Henry T. Kaiser),
25 (Sipa), 27 (Reso), 29 (Lehtikuva). Steve Gorton: 4, 16, 18, 26, 28. Cover: Corbis/Larry
Williams (main image), Corbis (front inset, centre right), Steve Gorton (back, front
inset far left), Digital Vision (front insets centre left, far right). Illustration page 5:
Jim Robins.

Contents

On the move

To swim, you move your arms and legs. You push yourself through the water by sweeping your arms backward and kicking with your legs.

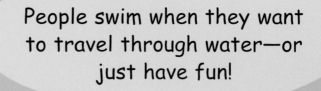

People swim when they want to travel through water—or just have fun!

4

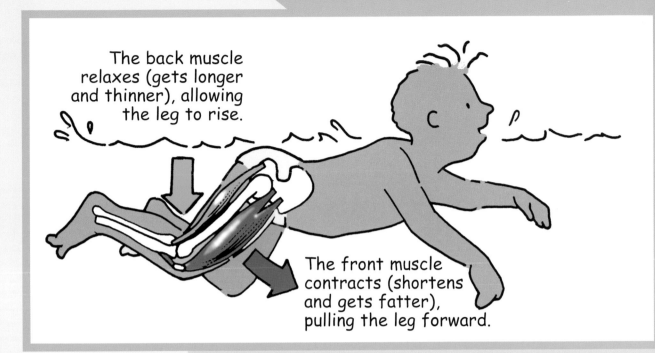

The back muscle relaxes (gets longer and thinner), allowing the leg to rise.

The front muscle contracts (shortens and gets fatter), pulling the leg forward.

Muscles work in pairs. One muscle contracts while the other muscle relaxes. In this way, muscles move bones in your skeleton forward to help you to swim.

You use many **muscles** when you swim. Muscles move the bones at the joints, such as those in your legs and arms.

Muscles cannot push. They can only pull.

Diving

One of the best ways to get into the water is to dive. You stretch your arms out so that the body becomes more streamlined.

Some swimmers dive into the water from a platform or board.

A penguin dives into the sea head first. Penguins cannot fly, but they are very good swimmers.

A penguin pushes itself along by using its wings as **flippers**.

Penguins have thick layers of fat that keep them warm in the icy sea.

swimming along

Most people swim along on the top of the water. They stay near the surface so that they can **breathe**. People cannot breathe underwater.

Olympic swimmers can reach speeds of 5 miles an hour (8 km/h).

A triathlon is a race where people swim, cycle, and run against each other.

Hippopotamuses swim just like they walk. They move their legs backward and forward, pushing their way through the water.

A hippopotamus keeps its eyes and ears out of the water as it swims.

Turning round

Good swimmers can turn round very quickly at the end of a pool. They turn a **somersault** in the water, then push off from the side with their feet.

Once a swimmer has pushed off from the side, he moves forward several feet under water.

A shark has a large **fin** on its tail.
It uses this to turn round, moving it
to one side like the rudder of a ship.

Sharks have to keep swimming or they will sink to the bottom.

When a shark swims near the surface, its tail fin sticks out the water. You can see the danger coming.

Breathing underwater

You can swim just below the surface of water using a snorkel—a breathing tube. This allows you to breathe in and out without taking your head out of the water.

The swimmer wears a mask over her nose and mouth.

Fish can breathe underwater. They have **gills** that get the **oxygen** they need from the water.

A fish gulps in water through its mouth. The water passes over its gills and out through openings either side of its head.

Most fish cannot breathe when they are out of the water.

Diving deep

People who swim deep under the water have to wear special tanks so they can breathe. The tanks contain air, which the swimmer breathes in through a tube.

Flippers help divers to move quickly through the water.

Deep-sea divers wear a special diving suit. This keeps them warm when they are swimming at the bottom of the cold sea.

Whales are mammals not fish. They come to the surface to breathe air. A sperm whale can stay underwater for as long as 75 minutes.

Whales dive very deep to find food. They like to eat squid and many kinds of **shellfish**.

Floating

You do not have to swim all the time in the water. You can lie on your back, spread out your arms, and float.

You can use a plastic float to help support the weight of your body.

Otters spend many hours a day in rivers and streams, looking for fish and shellfish to eat. To rest and relax, they float in the water.

When otters are swimming, they can keep their ears and nostrils closed.

The sea otter often swims on its back. Mothers carry baby otters on their chests as they paddle about.

Splashing

Do you like to splash people with water? You can splash by kicking with your legs, or by smacking the water with your hands.

When you swim using the butterfly stroke, both arms hit the water at the same time.

Splashing is fun, and it can also help to **exercise** your muscles.

A goose splashes a lot when it is bathing. It thrashes its wings in the water to clean its feathers.

Geese have very big and strong wings that they sometimes flap to frighten away enemies.

Crossing water

Some people swim to get across a pool or river or to race. They swim in a straight line from one side across to the other.

The distance from one side of a swimming pool to the other is called a width. The distance from one end to the other is called a length.

A swan swims across a pond to reach the other side. It paddles with its webbed feet below the surface of the water.

Swans produce a special oil for their feathers that protects them against the coldness of the water.

Swans' wings are made of fine, light bones covered in feathers to help them to glide across water.

Swimming together

You can have a great time swimming with your friends in the sea or in a pool. You can throw a ball, race against each other, or just have a good splash.

Playing in a swimming pool is good fun and good exercise.

Some schools contain hundreds of millions of fish.

A female herring lays up to 180,000 eggs at a time.

Fish live and swim together in huge groups called schools or shoals. They keep close to each other to protect themselves against enemies.

Swimming fast

The fastest kind of swimming is called the crawl. The swimmer breathes by turning their head to one side as their arm goes over.

There are four main kinds of swimming stroke: front crawl, breaststroke, backstroke, and butterfly.

In a race, the competitors swim in lanes, separated by ropes.

The sailfish swims by swinging its strong tail from side to side. This gives it the thrust to go forward. It steers and keeps balance using its sail—the tall fin on it's back.

The sailfish is the fastest moving fish. It swims at more than 62 miles an hour (100 km/h).

Swimming slowly

If you feel tired swimming, you can slow down. Or you can stay in the same place by treading water (kicking downward with your feet).

The slower you swim, the more likely you will sink.

The jellyfish swims very slowly. It moves by opening and closing its body, rather like an umbrella, to squeeze water out from underneath.

Some jellyfish are very dangerous. Poison from a sea wasp jellyfish can kill a person in three minutes.

As a jellyfish sinks, it catches small creatures with its stinging tentacles.

Getting out

When you get out of the water at a swimming pool, you will be very wet. You should tread carefully so that you don't slip over.

It is important not to get too cold after you have been swimming.

Most dogs love getting wet and are very good swimmers. They can dive in the water and climb out like humans.

Most dogs swim by paddling all four legs together. People "doggy paddle" when they flap their arms and legs in the water like a dog.

Dogs dry their coats by shaking their body hard or by rolling on the grass.

Facts and figures

The slowest of all fish is the tiny seahorse, which swims at only 40 feet an hour (0.016 km/h).

The deepest recorded dive by an animal is 1594 feet (483 m), by an Emperor penguin of the Antarctic. It is likely that whales can dive much deeper than this—to about 8250 feet (2500 m).

The deepest dive by a person with breathing equipment is about 1700 feet (520 m).

The largest fish in the world is a whale shark, which can reach 43 feet (13 m) in length and weigh 15 tons (about 15 tonnes).

Submersibles, which are craft specially built to take people deep underwater, have reached depths of 36,000 feet (10,916 m).

The long-distance champion of all the animals is the Loggerhead turtle. Scientists believe that it swims over 15,000 miles (24,000 km) in a year from Mexico to Japan and back.

The fastest human swimmer is Alexander Popov of Russia. In 2000 he won a 55-yard (50-m) race in only 21.64 seconds—that's nearly 6 miles an hour (9 km/h).

Words to remember

Breathe To take fresh air into the body and to get rid of used air. People breathe with their lungs. Fish breathe with gills.

Exercise Regular activity, for example walking, running, swimming. To do a sport or pastime that gets your muscles, lungs, and heart working hard.

Fin A sticking-out part of the body of a fish and some other water animals that helps them balance or change direction.

Flipper A flat, paddle-like part of the body used in swimming.

Gills Parts of a fish or amphibian (frog, toad, newt) in the neck that takes in oxygen from water.

Joint A part of the skeleton where two bones meet.

Muscle A bundle of elastic-like fibers that can tighten or relax to move parts of an animal or person's body.

Oxygen A gas contained in the air that all living things need to stay alive.

Shellfish Seafood, such as oysters and mussels, which have a hard shell.

Somersault A head-over-heels leap or roll, in water or on the ground.

Index